Shipping Container Homes

How to build a shipping container home, including plans, cool ideas, and more!

Table of Contents

Introduction

I want to thank you and congratulate you for picking up the book, "Shipping Container Homes".

This is the recently updated 2nd edition of this title. In response to feedback, this book has been totally re-created. New chapters and sections have been added, and it's been greatly improved.

This book contains helpful information about shipping container homes, what they are, and how to build one. You will learn about the different methods used to create a home using shipping containers, different styles of homes, and the different professionals you will need to work with.

Shipping container homes are a cheap, attractive, and unique alternative to building a regular house. Creating a shipping container home has a huge range of benefits, and can be a really enjoyable project.

This book includes great tips and techniques that will help you to create your very own shipping container home in no time! It also includes a few sample container home plans, along with some great unique ideas for your container home.

Thanks again for taking the time to read this book, good luck with your building project, and I hope you find this book to be helpful!

Chapter 1:
Shipping Container Home Building 101

Strong, inexpensive, and ultra versatile, steel containers are fast replacing traditional building materials. These containers are commonly used for storage and deliveries of items, but people are discovering that they can also be used as shelters. Thus, container homes are now becoming the trend in modern living, and it's no surprise that you have heard about them and become interested in acquiring one yourself.

Container houses are fairly easy to build. You simply need to purchase a shipping/cargo container, plan the sections of your home, acquire materials, and hire a few people to help you out. There are few things needed for container homes. In contrast, traditional ones require a variety of materials such as wooden panels, steel sheets, frames, bricks, etc. just to create a basic form. Because of its simplicity, a container home costs less and is built sooner than a regular home.

You can also turn a container house into a mobile home by attaching it to a vehicle. After all, containers are designed to be mobile so they are easily transportable. Because of these and other benefits, more and more people are now living in container homes.

This book will guide you in the methods of building a container home. Before going on to the specifics however, here are some frequently asked questions and the answers to them:

<u>**FAQ**</u>

What is a shipping container?

A shipping container is a large steel box. It is also known as a sea container, cargo container, freight container, hi-cube container box, and ISO container. These containers are mainly used for storing and delivering items, but recently, they have been converted into temporary or permanent shelters as well. You will usually spot them on a truck, train, ship, or stacked along port areas and storage facilities.

What makes a shipping container good for building a home?

Shipping containers have the following characteristics:

- Inexpensive. Building a shipping container home costs less than constructing a non-container house of the same size - in some cases, costs are down by about 50% or more.

- Versatile. A shipping container is easily modifiable. You can cut holes in one to make doors and windows, put containers side by side or on top of each other, and more. A container house can also serve as a mobile home.

- Easy to build. The main body of the house (the container) is already available so you'll have a finished home sooner. You also reduce planning because you work with the dimensions of the container instead of building from scratch.

- Durable. Storage containers are designed to be strong – they are put under a series of tests such as machine pulling, dropping from a great height, and so on. Only those that pass these tests are distributed in the market. Container buildings can be made to withstand natural disasters; a plus if you're living in a disaster-prone location.

- Availability. Shipping containers are in abundant supply so you won't have to worry about running out of materials.

- Environment-friendly. Reusing a shipping container as a home will help reduce pollution in the planet. It will also save a lot of trees from being cut.

- Unique. Container homes are fairly new so yours will be interesting at least.

Are these steel containers resistant to corrosion?

Shipping containers, especially ISBU, are built to withstand corrosion brought about by humidity, rain, and seawater. However, the anti-corrosion treatment wears off after some time. Expect newer containers to have higher resistance against corrosive elements. Even though the container may already have been pretreated for corrosion, you would still have to use anti-corrosive products from time to time. Spraying insulation coating on both sides of the container walls will also help.

How can I use shipping containers to build a home?

Containers form the main body of a home. Their parts are modified to enable people to stay inside them. Here is how people can convert a container into a living space:

- Cut out doors and windows in a container to turn it into a room

- Stack containers side by side or on top of each other for multi-level or multi-sectional homes

- Join containers together to form bigger rooms

Here are some arrangement ideas for multiple containers:

- Side by side or stacked

- L shaped – with a short extension on one side

- Equal sized containers at right angles from each other

- Parallel and joined together but with one slightly ahead of the other

- A long container stacked on top of a shorter one, and vice versa

- Two containers spaced apart from each other but joined under a single roof

- One or multiple containers underground

- Two containers parallel to each other but with a space in between them

- U shaped arrangement composed of two long parallel containers and one short one linking them at one side

- Two containers set apart from each other with one container lying on both these containers

Although containers can take on various arrangements, they need to be structurally stable in order to be safe. You may have seen container homes with wild designs, but you can be sure that they are carefully planned out and inspected before they are built. Building these homes is regulated by building codes. If you're interested in having an unconventionally-designed home, work with an architect or structural engineer and seek the approval of a building authority. Doing this will help you avoid problems later on.

What sizes do shipping containers come in?

Common sizes are as follows:

- Length: 20 feet, 40 feet

- Width: 8 feet

- Heights: 8 feet 6 inches (regular) and 9 feet 6 inches (Hi-cube)

Ask the provider of the shipping container to give you a blueprint of their product. This will greatly help you later on during the designing and building process.

How heavy is a shipping container?

An empty 20 ft shipping container typically weighs 2,500 kilograms, a 30ft container weighs 3,000 kilograms, and a 40ft container weighs 4, 400 kilograms. Because of this, you need to rent heavy-duty moving equipment for working with one.

How much weight can a shipping container carry?

A container can safely support up to 67,200 kilograms, but ask the provider to be sure.

How will I move the shipping container to my chosen location?

Shipping containers are delivered via trucks which have cranes attached to them; they will be lifted onto the ground where they will be used. Vehicles that are often used for this purpose are roll bed trailers, boom trucks, and excavators. If the delivery vehicle doesn't have a crane, a forklift may be used to get the containers on and off it.

Be forewarned that while shipping container companies may provide the delivery service, they may limit the areas where they will deliver the containers to. You might have to convince them to deliver to certain locations or hire somebody else to do the job. Deliveries are often computed per mile.

You need enough space for setting up the container – twice the container's length plus an allowance of 10 feet. 75 feet of cleared space will usually do. This is to make sure that there will be enough room to maneuver the container/s.

A crane or an excavator may be used to position containers. If you intend to set up a container at a temporary location and move it with a jack, make sure that it is propped up with pipes, tires or other heavy-duty materials. This will allow a jack to fit under it and lift it.

You can also move the container for short distances without using a crane. Use a jack to lift the container, and insert thick steel pipes underneath. This will enable the container to roll.

You may attach a rope to the front or back of the container and pull it manually or with a pick-up truck.

What is a good location for a shipping container home?

A good location for a home in general is on stable ground and on safe property. Look for the following characteristics in an area:

- Sturdy soil not prone to liquefaction

- Dry and level surface, preferably with concrete or pavement

Note: If the surface is uneven, spacers made of durable material may be placed under the shipping container's corners to adjust its position.

How do I get a shipping container?

You can find shipping containers in the following places:

- Ports. The container home site doesn't need to be near a port. Shipping containers may be delivered to a particular location. However, if the port is far away such as from overseas, expect to wait months before the container arrives.

- Areas near a port. You can usually find distributors of shipping containers in these places.

- Online search. Use a web browser to search for ISO containers, shipping containers, cargo containers, intermodal containers, or freight containers. Add the location where you intend to buy them from. This will limit the search results to those which are available on the place you specify. Also, adding the phrase 'for sale' directs you to the pages where they are actually sold and filter out irrelevant material.

- Online shopping websites. The advantage of using these sites is that you can compare prices and read reviews.

- Classified ads. Shipping containers are sometimes sold on classified ads.

- Phone book. Contact shipping businesses and ask if they are selling containers. They are listed under shipping and freight.

What Kind of Container Do I Buy?

There are many kinds of shipping containers. The 20 feet and the 40 feet containers are the most frequently used for container homes, but there are also other containers that measure 10 feet in length and half the height of regular containers (around 4 feet or so). High cube containers are higher than the regular containers.

Containers may have collapsible sides (flat rack container), have an open top (open top container), have doors on both of its ends (tunnel container), or have doors on its sides (open side container). Choose the container dimensions and types that are well suited for your home design.

Shipping containers are designed to be reused – remember this and expect that a container you are interested with may have been previously used before. Generally, used containers are cheaper than brand new ones. The more used they are, the cheaper they get, and the more damage they may have sustained. Because of this, seek ISO (International Standard

Organization) containers. They are built according to strict standards and will be of higher quality compared to other types of steel containers.

Are you looking for the cheapest container to buy? You must know that the difference of price between a second hand container and a brand new one may not be that great. If you're choosing between a new and old container, it's best to go for the new one because it is often cleaner and stronger.

Check the status of the container if you can before buying. Shipping container ads may not give complete details. Evaluate the container personally and see if it matches your expectations and requirements. By seeing the container yourself, you will know firsthand if it will be suitable for your building plans. Bring along a structural engineer with you so he/she can tell you whether the item is reliable or not.

Going to the container may not be possible especially if you're ordering from overseas. If this is the case, ask someone you trust to go to the location and send you pictures.

A container usually has data plates attached to it. You will find the following information on these:

- Date of manufacture

- Manufacturer

- Previous user

- Security seals – look for these to know if the container has passed quality checks

Ask for additional information such as what it was previously used for and how long it has been used already. Tell the seller that you intend to use it as living space. Take care not to buy a container that was used to store hazardous items such as chemicals, trash, and other items that may damage and leave traces on the container. The cleaning and repairing costs may not be worth it. Smells may also linger long after the materials are dealt with - this is risky especially if there is an asthmatic in the family. Ensure that you get a clean and safe container to avoid putting yourselves in danger.

Is building a shipping container home complicated?

Container home construction is not that complicated. Building one can be compared to working on a steel building. If you can find some people who have experience in steel building construction, you will have people who can work with you.

Do I need to get permits for this?

Shipping containers that are used as shelters temporarily do not usually require a permit. If you plan to live in it for the long term, you will need planning permission for it. Talk with the local building authority to acquire permits.

Chapter 2:
Planning Your Shipping Container Home

Plans are essential in building a container house. By planning, you streamline your efforts and prepare adequately. You see potential problems and create the solutions to them before they even occur. Your plans will also matter in whether you get building permits or not. This is why you should do your best to create thorough plans.

General Design Plan

Formulate a general design for your home. Doing these things will help you in designing your home by immersing yourself to container home possibilities. Some ways to get ideas are:

- Looking at photos and designs of shipping container homes

- Use programs for designing a shipping container home. You can find some of these on the Internet.

- Personally going to an actual shipping container and exploring it to get a sense of how living in one will be like

- Going to a shipping container home and talking to the people who live there or who have designed it

Think about how you would want to live inside your home. What do you want your house to contain so that it would allow you to live how you want? Estimate how much space you need for each partition of the home.

You may have to adjust your goals based on the following:

- Your budget

- The site where you intend to build your home

- The available spaces within and around the container

- Building guidelines and restrictions

- Available materials

To make it easier, get assistance from the following people:

- Shipping home owners and architects

- Design experts

- Contractors

- Modular shipping container home professionals

- Shipping container modifiers

- Structural engineers

- Civil engineers

- Suppliers of materials and equipment for shipping container homes

- Building department personnel in the locality – to know site servicing requirements and codes

Talk with as many of these people as you can so you can get a competitive price, refine your designs, and solve problems related to construction.

Location Plan

Find ideal spots for construction. Take into consideration the following things:

- Views of the surrounding

- Soil bearing and grade

- Landscape. You can do landscaping, but you can save costs if you work with the preexisting landscape.

- Shading. Trees, landscape, and surrounding structures contribute to shading. These will help with temperature control.

- Nearness to boundaries and roads. You need to consider these to allocate enough space between your home and its surroundings.

- Location in the neighborhood. Are you near amenities such as groceries, hospitals, and the like?

Hire a real estate agent to make it easier for you to locate ideal spots. If you can't pick one, consider having a mobile home instead.

Interior Design Plan

Get the maximum square footage that is available for your home. Your architect, engineer, or designer will assist you with this. Getting exact measurements will refine your designs.

Before designing though, know the rules of building your home. Compliance to these rules is important so you can build the home and live in it legally. Thus, your plan must include gathering details about building codes and requirements, fulfilling them, and talking with the building authority in your locality.

Constructing Your House Floor Plan

If you don't have the measurements of the shipping container yet, get them using a tape measure. Record the numbers for later – you'll need them to make an accurate house floor plan.

A floor plan has measurements that are to scale. You can use graphing paper for this. Draw the outline of the container and add things like partitions, entrances, windows, and furniture. If you have preexisting items to add, you must measure them first so you can fit them in the plan properly.

Designate the number and types of rooms you plan to construct, along with estimates of square footage for each. Ask help from your architect. You can also use shipping container home design programs – you'll find them online.

Design Details

A single container may suffice for a shelter. Windows and doors may be created out of the walls by cutting the metal. The pre-existing container doors are kept intact to allow for expansion of the shelter, but they may be removed and replaced by slider doors.

The body of the container provides the following:

- Roof

- Floor

- Walls

You will need to add these to the main body:

Windows

Choose the location of the windows carefully to achieve proper ventilation and ideal temperature in the shipping container. This is important especially if you will rely on passive temperature maintenance. Take advantage of existing trees and shading – these will cut your expenses that will otherwise be spent on active heating and cooling.

Windows are formed by cutting holes out of the metal walls using a reciprocating saw. Pre-made windows are then fitted on the hole and supported by a platform (preferably steel) measuring at least 2 inches wide.

Doors

The ends of containers may have doors already, but you can cut out additional doors on its sides. The steel container doors may also be modified by adding traditional-style doors.

Skylights

It's easy to install skylights in a shipping container home because of its small size. As much as possible though, do not damage the water-tight roof when doing roof modifications. Along with this, reroute pipes and vents through the walls. This will help you avoid having to get additional waterproofing for your roof.

Paneling

Paneling the walls for decorative purposes is optional. Otherwise, the steel walls can stand on their own.

Insulation

Shipping container homes can be a little challenging to insulate. However, you will be able to do it with the right tools.

You can use spray-on insulation products to coat both inside and outside of the container walls. Examples are insulation paint and polyurethane foam. These contain air bubbles that absorb heat and reduce the tendency of metal to heat or cool down very quickly. Some of these are also waterproof and will protect your container from corrosion.

Roll-on insulation, such as mineral wool, will also work. Before using a material for insulation, check whether these are safe for the material of the container. Some items commonly used for insulating homes are corrosive. They also tend to trap moisture and keep them close to the walls, which may result in structural damage over time.

Insulation can take up a few inches from the sides and top of the container, so adjust your floor plan accordingly. The floor usually has the thickest insulation layer, followed by the roof, and the walls the thinnest.

Heating and Cooling

Temperature regulation will depend on the following factors: shape and size of the container/s, the orientation of the structure, wall and surface materials, and insulation. Make the most out of the natural environment to cut expenses from active thermal regulation. Position the container on a site with trees that block the cold wind and the hot sunlight. Foliage on the south and west of the house will do great. Aside from these passive thermal regulation methods, you can also install active thermal regulation systems such as heaters and air conditioners. Just make sure to include layouts and details of these systems in your documentation.

Framework

Framework is important for providing support to parts of the container, especially if it has undergone extensive modifications. Steel frames are ideal for container homes but pretreated wood will also suffice.

Supports

Specially treated decking lumber and/or heavy-duty connecting hardware provide support for roofs and partitions that are external to the main body of the container. Steel I-beam frameworks are often used to support a split-level container home. These are linked together with self-anchoring screws and bolts.

Foundations

A shipping home's foundations can be slab on grade application constructed from precast concrete panels or concrete. Excavate the perimeter and fill the trench with gravel to allow for drainage. The foundation walls are fortified by back-filling, soil compaction, rebars, etc. Utilities are installed along the base of the foundations and towards their designated locations. Foundation costs will be affected by the quality of the soil and the slope of the land, so choose your site wisely.

Foundation Footings

Prevent moisture from accumulating at the base of the cylinder by keeping the container at least 12 inches above the ground. Footings may be made of cylindrical/square concrete pieces or railroad ties. If you use wooden footings, place gravel under them to drain off water and prevent it from damaging the wood.

Poured concrete footings are best but heavy steel jack stands will work as well. Do not use bricks and cinder block as foundation materials. These are prone to cracking. These footings should measure no less than 2 inches wide.

These are placed under the ends of the shipping container. Do not place footings at the middle because these may deform the structure. After all, the edges of the container are the ones that are bearing the weight.

Flooring

Shipping containers usually have plywood floors. Choose those with at least a 1.5-inch hardwood flooring. This can be used for the floor, but thinner plywood may be placed on top of it for additional strength.

Utilities

Like with regular homes, you will need the assistance of utility personnel to install utility lines in your home safely and legally:

- Electricity

- Gas

- Telephone and internet cables

- Plumbing (piped-in water, sewage and run-off)

On the other hand, you may decide to live off-the-grid and not have utilities connected to your house. A shipping container can be connected to a vehicle, turning it into a mobile home. This may or may not have traditional utilities. For example, there are container homes that use rainwater harvesting systems, solar-powered electrical systems, and the likes.

Chapter 3:
Acquiring Permits

You will be asked to submit these before you will be given a permit to build your home:

- Soil report

- Land surveys

- Elevation

- Energy code compliance

- Water treatment

Aside from that, prepare the following documents:

- Architectural Plans

- Structural Plans

- Mechanical Plans

- Electrical Plans

These documents need to be stamped and signed by a licensed professional.

Architectural Documentation

These include the address of the container home, floor plans of rooms with doors and windows showing, exterior elevations, diagrams and details of foundations, floors, walls, stairs, basements, plumbing fixtures, and other features, and compliance to wall-bracing and energy code requirements.

Structural Documentation

These include uniform and special loads, foundation plans, ventilation and openings, floor and roof framing, supports, renovations, additions, and other structural details.

Mechanical Documentation

These include heating and cooling load computations, as well as ventilation layouts.

Electrical

The electrical system of your home will be inspected. Present plans for the electrical system in your home – these include the riser diagram and a list of electrical equipment.

Contract Documents

Contract documents are drawings and specifications for all the systems and parts of the home. The contractor needs these to know how much to charge you, obtain the required permits, coordinate with other people for services and materials, and accomplish the project. Even if you don't have a contractor and you plan on building your home yourself, you will still need to make these documents to guide you in what to do.

Discuss your plans and documentation with a building official to gain permits. Then, discuss these documents with potential contractors and get pricing for materials and services. Determine what container modifications and fittings will be needed, and decide whether they will be done on site or from a factory.

Chapter 4:
Container Home Modifications

A shipping container has a monocoque body, meaning that its external part supports the load it contains. All its parts play a role in maintaining its integrated structure. It is strong as it is, and it can withstand loads that are heavier than those present in usual home construction. However, it becomes weakened when its structures are modified such as when holes are cut, paneling is removed, etc. Because of this, you will need a structural architect and/or engineer if you plan to change the components of the container. Such a professional will determine whether the modification is feasible and formulate designs to make it so.

Generally, if you remove panels from the container, you will need to install steel frames to make up for lost support. Also, additional columns and supportive structures may be required for roofs, door frames, window openings, and other components that were not originally found in the container.

Working with steel is common in shipping container home construction. To save on expenses, it is better if the cutting, welding and reinforcing is done in the factory. Fittings are done on-site.

Attaching the Containers

Containers are clamped together with specialized IC clamps. If these are not available, ¼ inch steel plates or coil spring compressors may be used. These attachments are welded on the corners.

Cutting the Container

Ensure that the containers are linked together securely before cutting down sections of the walls. The containers' edges are their strongest points and these carry the bulk of the weight. If you intend to attach multiple containers together, make sure that they are securely attached to one another at their edges so they can evenly distribute the load. If they're not linked adequately, cutting the supporting walls between them will throw off the balance and cause the structure to collapse. Again, these containers need to be joined only at the corners and edges.

A reciprocating saw is used to cut the corrugated steel of the shipping container. Plot the cuts with a marker and drill holes in the corners as starting points cutting the metal.

Joining Items Together

Linking components can involve clamps, screws, bolts, metal plates, and other connecting hardware. Welding may be done with metal parts. Construction adhesives may be used to avoid drilling holes unnecessarily.

Sealing Seams

Seams may be joined together with galvanized steel roofing material and sealed together with hot tar.

Chapter 5:
Shipping Home Container Design Ideas

As mentioned in the first chapter, container homes can have multiple arrangements. A single container may be enough for a home, but several can also be combined. These containers can be put on top of each other or side by side in various orders. Here are some things you can do with these containers:

Apartments

Several containers stacked together will make up a several-storied apartment.

House with Patio

A multi-level house may be composed of 2 containers stacked on top of each other, and a third one lying next to them. The roof of the bottom container will serve as the patio. A staircase may be installed to allow people to climb to the patio from the outside.

Underground Shelter or Basement

Use an excavator to dig up enough soil for a container to fit inside. Pretreat the container with anti-corrosive substances such as boat paint. Lower the container into the hole with a crane. Pour gravel into the spaces left between the container and the soil around it to protect the container walls. If the structure is completely underground and windowless, install roof vents.

Vehicle Parking Space

A 40 feet Hi-Cube container can accommodate a mini garage. It can also be used for a vehicle repair workstation. For tall vehicles such as sailboats or trucks, use Hi-Cube containers and a high roof supported by metal frameworks.

Tunnel

Put one roof over two single containers with a space in between them. This will create a parking area or a tunnel to let vehicles and people park through.

Flood Proofing

To flood proof your home, you may use 5 inch I-beam frameworks to lift the container off of the ground. Support these with footings and bolts.

Solar Powered Home

The roof of a container home may have solar panels attached to it. They are usually angled away from the top of the roof to allow for ventilation and water drainage. Having these panels will greatly help in saving money on electric bills. It might require an initial investment that is worth more than being connected to the electricity company, but it will pay off and save you money in the long term. Also, having solar panels instead of an electrical connection enables mobility.

Rainwater Collection System

The roof of the container home may have a rainwater catching system to provide for water requirements. The water collected may be filtered and distributed to the pipes in the home. It's important to note that this may not be safe for drinking, but can be used for washing, flushing the toilet, etc. However, the collected water may be passed through a high-grade filter to become safe enough to drink.

Pool

You can use a shipping container as a swimming pool. The container is coated with an anti-corrosive product such as boat paint and water sealant for it to be used this way.

Mobile Home

A shipping container may be attached to a large truck to enable movement. Utilities can be attached and detached with this kind of home.

To Sum It Up:

Building a shipping container home involves the following:

- Making designs
- Consulting professionals
- Refining designs
- Getting permits and passing inspections
- Coordinating with contractors
- Acquiring materials
- Building the container
- Getting final permits and a certificate of occupancy

There you have it! Have fun building your own shipping container home.

Chapter 6:
Shipping Container Home Budget

One of the benefits of having a shipping container home is the lowered cost of creation, but just how much exactly do these homes cost to build?

Obviously, this depends on a few different factors. When trying to determine your budget, you have to ask yourself a few questions:

- How big do I want my container home to be?

- Do I want a multi-level container home?

- Do I want to add features such as a swimming pool?

- What kind of finish do I want in my container home? (e.g. types of flooring)

- Will I be building the container home myself?

- Will I be hiring contractors for some parts of the job?

- Will I be outsourcing the entire building project?

- Do I want multiple designs to be drawn up by an architect?

- What government, council, and connection fees will I have to pay?

- Are shipping containers readily available in my area?

- Will I be buying new containers or second hand ones?

All of these factors and more can affect the total cost of your build. While shipping container homes are relatively cheap to build, if you're planning to build a mansion with elaborate designs and fittings, the costs will still add up.

One of the primary costs involved is purchasing the shipping container itself. This cost depends on the type of container you'd like, the amount of containers you'll be needing, and if you're buying them second hand or brand new. The shipping containers can also fluctuate greatly in price depending on where you're located. For obvious reasons, shipping containers will generally be cheaper and more readily available to those in large coastal areas.

You can find some second hand shipping containers for as inexpensively as $1500. On the other hand, some of the more expensive, brand new containers may cost $7000+.

You do also need to be careful about the quality of container you're purchasing. Don't always jump at the cheapest deal. It may not be safe to build with, depending on what it's carried, and it may carry an unsavory odor.

Because there are so many variables involved, it's impossible to tell you exactly how much your particular container home would cost. Instead, let's take a look at a couple of comparable figures, and see how shipping container homes stack up next to conventionally build houses.

Example 1: Bungalow

Size = 215 square feet (2 Containers used)

Conventional build cost = $80,000

Shipping container build cost = $35,000

Example 2: 3 Bedroom home, 2 levels

Size: 2560 square feet (8 containers used)

Conventional build cost = $280,000

Shipping container build cost = $145,000

As you can see in the above examples, the costs can vary. These are both real examples from around the world, with actual cost figures. Things can also be built more cheaply, or more expensively. It really depends upon how you answered the earlier questions regarding the build.

If you want to build a giant container home, the costs will clearly rise. However, as you can see in comparison with the conventional builds the prices are a lot cheaper (often around 50%). Not only that, the shipping container homes are a lot quicker to construct than a conventional house.

As you can tell, shipping container homes do make a lot of sense. They're environmentally friendly, attractive, unique, quick to build, and a lot of fun to design and create!

Chapter 7:
The Actual Building Process

Having a shipping container home obviously has some amazing benefits. It's something that a lot of people are interested in, and is obviously why you're reading this book in the first place.

There comes a crucial point however where you must decide if you would like to undertake the building process yourself, or use contactors to perform the build.

There are companies that will complete the entire process for you, and others that will simply work with you along the way.

Your decision ultimately comes down to your confidence in your building and management abilities, and your budget. To undertake a build like this you must have a certain amount of building skill and knowledge. You must be able to get building permits for your area, acquire the tools necessary, and have the skills to follow all of the steps in the building process.

If you're not comfortable doing the whole thing yourself, then you can obviously hire some contractors along the way to give you a hand with certain aspects (such as fitting windows), or you can hire a company to complete the entire thing for you. This will result in a faster build that is often of a higher quality if you're not actually a builder by trade, but will typically cost more overall, and you don't get the same satisfaction as you would if you completed the project on your own.

If you decide to build it yourself, you need to follow the following steps.

Step 1: Design

At this stage, you will start by brainstorming the basic ideas of your container home, the size it should be, and what it should include.

How many rooms would you like? How big should it be? What features should it include? This is where you answer all of these questions. You can then start drawing out sample ideas, or base your designs off of pre-existing plans.

A great tool to use is SketchUp which allows you to draw in 3D. It's commonly used for designing regular homes but you can also obviously use it for shipping container homes to get a better idea of how the finished product will look. You can check it out at www.sketchup.com

Once you have the plans figured out, you will need to see an architect or builder to help you finalize the plans and have them professionally drawn up. The architect will be able to tell you which of your plans are possible structurally, and will often have some great suggestions for various improvements. Once you have your official plans drawn up, it's on to the next stage.

Step 2: Lay the Foundation

You will need a solid foundation to build your container home on, just like any regular home. Unless you are a professional in this field, it's best to hire a contractor for this job. You need to make sure that the foundation is done correctly, with areas set out for the plumbing to be fitted.

If you're planning a poured concrete foundation, it's a good idea to embed steel fittings into the concrete where the corners of the shipping container will rest. This will help to support the container, but obviously consult with an engineer or architect about the best choice of foundation for your particular design.

Step 3: Purchase the Container/s

The next step will be purchasing the actual containers and having them delivered onsite. You need to choose between brand new containers vs. second hand, and also will have to choose a size of container that suits your plan.

Next, if your plan requires any extreme modification to your container, such as removing a large section of it, this should be done. If not, then it's time to place your shipping container on the foundation. This is best done with a crane which will obviously be one of the big expenses in the build. In some instances, you may also get away with using a forklift to maneuver the container.

At this point, your container is basically an empty shell, sitting on a solid foundation. Now it's time to really get to work to turning that empty container into a fully functioning home.

Step 4: Connect the Containers

Most likely, your home will consist of more than one container. At this point in time they will be simply sitting next to each other on your foundation, but won't be structurally attached.

The easiest way to attach these containers for DIYers is with a series of bolts drilled through the containers. This obviously isn't the strongest way to join the containers, but it's fast, inexpensive, and makes it possible to un-attach them in future if you want to make modifications. A stronger way to actually connect the containers would be through welding them together. If you connect the containers with bolts, you can always get them welded together later for a more structurally sounds build.

Step 5: Add Reinforcements

Before we remove any walls, we need to make sure that the building is structurally sound. This is where working with an engineer or architect is crucial. You also won't get a building approval unless you have the necessary reinforcements in place.

The necessary reinforcements will be totally different from house to house, and also depending on what your council's rules and regulations are. Normally it will consist of a certain number of steel beams that help to support the structure.

Unless you're a structural engineer, you should really seek professional advice in this area, otherwise the whole build will be compromised.

Step 6: Add a Roof

Depending on your plan, a roof may not even be necessary. It can however look great on a shipping container home, and help the proper run off from water. This is really helpful if you plan on installing a water tank as part of your design, as your roof can be made to collect the water.

It's easiest to add your roof prior to making any cut outs, while everything is still stable and connected. Be careful in designing your roof, and decide whether or not you'd like to add insulation. This can be a great way to add insulation to your container home, before the build really gets underway. You'll be able to live comfortably in one section of the home, while other parts are still being finished.

A simple shed-style roof is the easiest, allowing run-off from rain on both sides of the structure. Insulation can be easily fitted, and you can choose to either tile the roof, or simply add steel or tin sheeting as the roofing material.

Step 7: Cut outs

Now that you have your shell, it's time to cut out the openings for doorways and windows. Consult your plan, and mark out where the cuts should be made.

You can make these cuts with a cutting torch, a grinder, or a plasma cutter. If you want a clean finish, and are worried about charring the remaining walls and flooring, it's best to hire a welder for this job.

Also make sure to add holes necessary to fit any plumbing or gas fixtures.

Step 8: Add the Flooring

Now you need to add whatever flooring you'd like for your container.

Some people like to completely remove the existing flooring in the containers, whilst others like to simply cover it up. The choice is yours, and obviously depends on the particular container that you bought, and the plans that you are following.

A great choice for container homes is floating floorboards. They look like regular floorboards, but are fitted much more simply, almost like tiles. They're simple to look after, and give your container a real homely feel. But obviously, the choice is up to your personal preferences.

Step 9: Seal Cracks

There will be openings and cracks where the containers join that you have cut doorways. You'll need to seal these up and make sure the joins are clean.

One way to do this would be to weld them together once more. This is best done by a professional welder to ensure a flush finish.

A great thing to do at this point is to add foam insulation between the walls where the gaps are. Fill the gap with foam insulation, and either weld the joins shut afterwards, or use a foam sealant. Then you can want to add a backer rod and caulk to create a nice finish.

Step 10: Framing

It's now time to add wooden frames to the areas that you've cut. These are the areas where you'll be adding doorways and windows. If you don't have framing experience, it may be best to hire a builder.

You will be creating the frames and attaching them to the container. You can attach them through a combination of bolts and screws. Make sure that you use treated screws to ensure that they last and aren't corroded.

Step 11: Add Doors and Windows

Now that you've got all of your framing done, it's now a simple job of adding your doors and windows. Most people can purchase a pre-made door and fit it quite simply. Windows however can be quite a difficult skill. You will probably need to get the glass custom cut to fit your plan, and this requires a glazier. Then they will fit the windows for you.

Step 12: Interior Framing & Adding Dry Wall

Now that everything is structurally sound, sealed, and with doors and windows fitted, it's time to finish up the inside of your home. This framing should be quite simple to install, and is basically there to hold the dry wall in place.

Step 13: Wire Your Container Home

This is now the easiest point to wire your container home. This step does require an electrician. For obvious reasons, DO NOT try and do this yourself unless you're a licensed professional.

Add the wiring to all of the areas you need, then it's on to the next step.

Step 14: Insulate

You may have already added some insulation between the walls prior to sealing them up, and perhaps added some in your roof. It's a good idea to add additional insulation now to your walls, then you can finish up by hanging the dry wall.

You can also choose to insulate the exterior of your container home. It al depends on how you'd like it to look! If the exterior of your home will be covered with some type of cedar or vinyl finish, you can easily insulate beneath this finish.

Some people however, want their container home to look like a container on the outside, and display the steel wall of the original container. The choice is yours.

Step 15: Finishing Touches

Now your container home is pretty much complete. It's time to add the finishing touches. Get the final fittings added, such as toilets, sinks, air-conditioners, fans, and light-fittings. Once this is done, it's time to add furniture and move in — congratulations!

38

Chapter 8:
Sample shipping container home plans

In this chapter I've included a few sample shipping container home plans. These plans are just an example of what's possible. Use them for ideas, but ultimately it's best to create your own plan that you're going to love. Take bits from all of the plans you like, and start designing on your own to make a truly unique container home!

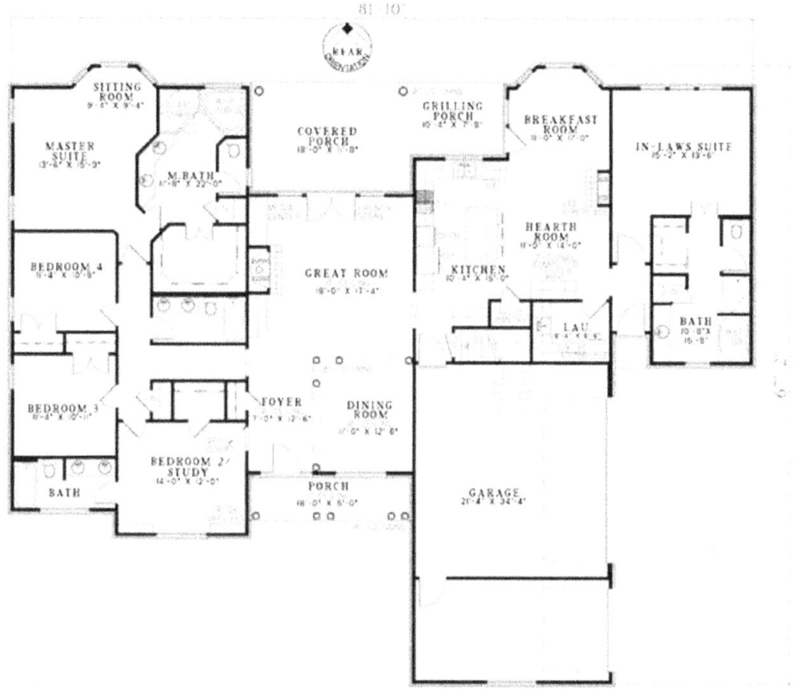

1 Bedroom Unit

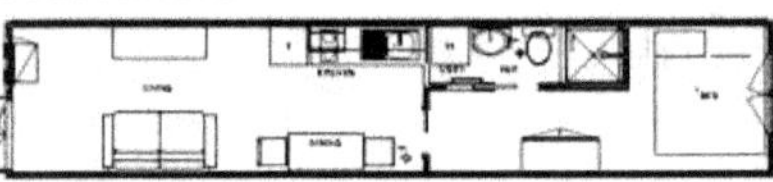

2 Bedroom Unit with Open Plan Living

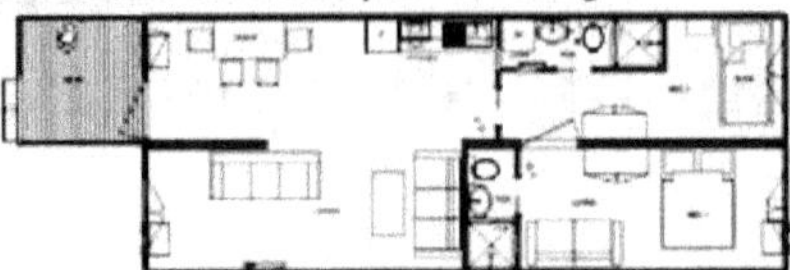

2 Bedroom Unit

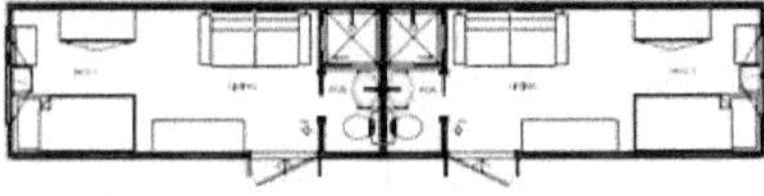

3 Bedroom Unit

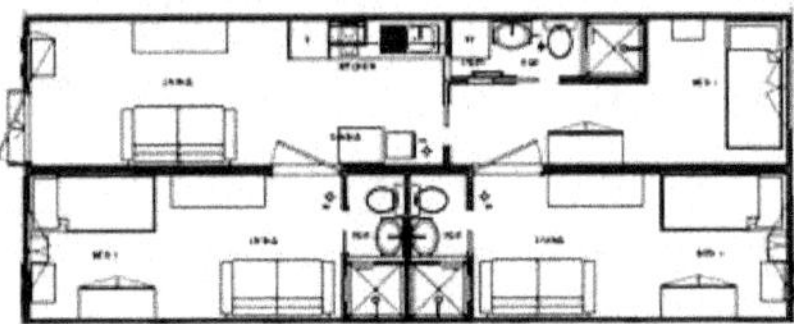

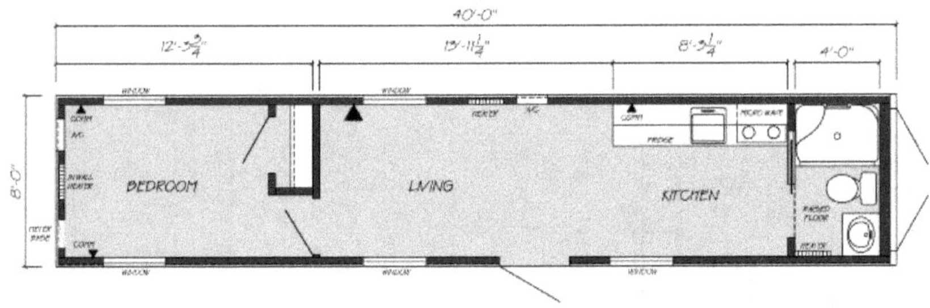

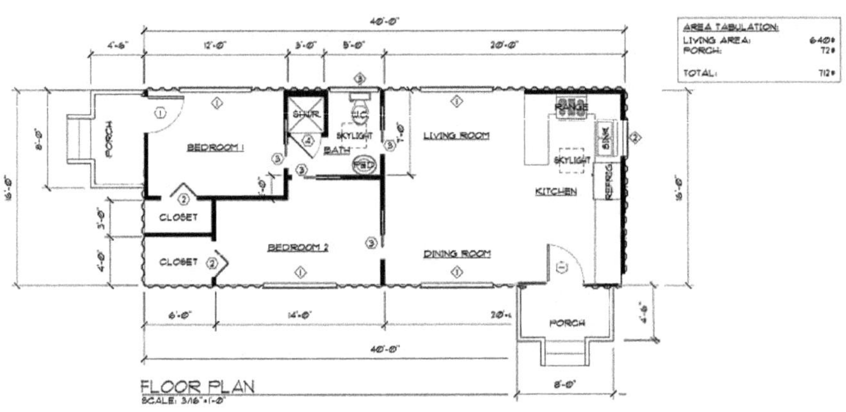

FLOOR PLAN
SCALE: 3/16"=1'-0"

Chapter 9:
Cool shipping container home ideas

If having a simple shipping container home isn't unique enough for you, there are plenty of things you can do to enhance it. This chapter will cover some of these ideas, and give you some food for thought in the design process.

Shipping Container Swimming Pool

One great addition you may want to consider, is a swimming pool. An old shipping container can be quite easily turned into a cool and unique pool.

The first thing you'll need to do is design the pool. Do you want it to be in-ground, or above-ground? How big would you like it to be? Where should it be located? You also need to consider how deep it should be. You may want to cut the walls of your container on a slant, so it's not too deep the whole way along.

Once you have a design in mind, it would be a great idea to consult with a structural engineer and get some official plans for your pool created. Next, you'll need to gain approval from your local council or government (depending where in the world you're located) before you can begin to build it.

Next up, it's time to ensure that your container is watertight and safe. This means you'll need to weld up any gaps or weaker areas in the design, add a sealant, and apply a rust-proof coating or paint.

The next stage is to add any plumbing and pumps required. At this stage you can consult with a local pool shop to get their advice, and possibly have someone help you with the plumbing installation.

Finally, you're ready to install your shipping container pool. This is a cheap and really cool way to create a swimming pool that perfectly matches your shipping container home!

Example of an in-ground shipping container pool

An above-ground shipping container pool

Solar Panels

A great addition to a shipping container home is solar panels. Container homes are already environmentally friendly, so why not make them more-so by adding some solar panels. These look nice, and also reduce the running costs of your container home. In lots of countries around the world right now, the installation of solar panels is subsidized by the government. Consult with your local government first, to see if you can get solar panels added at a lowered cost!

Water Tanks

You can also add a water tank to your container home. If you chose to have a slanted roof, you can set up your gutter system to collect the rainwater in a tank. You can either use a conventional water tank, or create your own out of a container!

This is similar to creating the pool, in that you will need to determine the size you want, seal it, clean it, and add the necessary plumbing. This can be a fun DIY project if you have some welding skills, and is another way to make your container home eco-friendly, self-sustaining, and reduce running costs!

Create Sky Lights

A great way to add light to your container home is to add sky lights. For a container home this is quite simple. Just cut out a section of the container home, and add in a panel of skylight glass!

These natural looking skylights are a great feature and help to naturally brighten up your home.

Chapter 10:
Resources

In this chapter I'd like to share some of my favorite websites for shipping container homes. On these websites you can find a lot of additional information that may be beyond the scope of this book, and many of these sites provide their own plans that I'm not allowed to legally put inside of this book.

These are some great resources for you during the design and troubleshooting process, so do be sure to check them out:

- http://www.containerhomeplans.org/

- http://www.residentialshippingcontainerprimer.com/

- http://www.containerhomes.net.au/

- http://homeinabox.blogspot.com.au/

- http://brightcontainerhouse.com/

- http://www.tincancabin.com/

- http://seacontainercabin.blogspot.com.au/

Conclusion

Thank you again for taking the time to read this book!

I hope this book was able to help you learn more about shipping container homes!

The next step is to put the strategies provided into use, and begin working on your own shipping container home!

Finally, if you enjoyed this book, please take the time to share your thoughts and post a review on Amazon. It'd be greatly appreciated!

Thank you and good luck!